What Is a Family?

Rebecca Rissman

www.heinemannraintree.com
Visit our website to find out
more information about
Heinemann-Raintree books.

To order:

☎ Phone 888-454-2279

🖥 Visit www.heinemannraintree.com
to browse our catalog and order online.

Edited by Rebecca Rissman, Daniel Nunn, and Harriet Milles
Designed by Joanna Hinton-Malivoire
Picture research by Tracy Cummins
Originated by Capstone Global Library Ltd.
Production by Victoria Fitzgerald
Printed and bound in China by Leo Paper Products Ltd

15 14 13 12 11
10 9 8 7 6 5 4 3 2 1

Library of Congress Cataloging-in-Publication Data
Rissman, Rebecca.
   What Is a family? / Rebecca Rissman.
      p. cm.
   Includes bibliographical references and index.
   ISBN 978-1-4329-5358-4 (hc)—ISBN 978-1-4329-5503-8 (pb) 1.
Families—Juvenile literature. I. Title.
   HQ744.R57 2012
   306.85—dc22   2010044802

Acknowledgments
The author and publishers are grateful to the following for permission
to reproduce copyright material: Corbis **p. 11** (© David P. Hall);
Getty Images **pp. 7** (Tim Hall), **15 right** (Stephen Simpson), **19**
(© Radius Images); istockphoto **pp. 5 left** (© RonTech2000),
6 (© Catherine Yeulet), **8** (© Silvia Jansen), **9** (© Joseph C.
Justice Jr.), **10** (© paul kline), **12** (© James Pauls), **13** (© Juhász
Péter), **14** (© Agnieszka Kirinicjanow), **16** (© Carmen Martínez
Banús); Shutterstock **pp. 4** (© Paul Prescott), **5 right**, **18** (©
iofoto), **15 left** (© BlueOrange Studio), **17**, **20** (© cabania), **21** (©
bikeriderlondon).

Front cover photograph of a family group reproduced with
permission of Getty Images (Anthony Plummer). Back cover
photographs reproduced with permission of istockphoto
(© Catherine Yeulet).

We would like to thank Anne Pezalla for her invaluable help in the
preparation of this book.

Every effort has been made to contact copyright holders of
material reproduced in this book. Any omissions will be rectified in
subsequent printings if notice is given to the publisher.

Some words appear in bold, **like this**. You can find out
what they mean in "Words to Know" on page 23.

Contents

About this series:
Books in this series introduce children to what families are, who can be family members, and how some people in families are related. Use this book to stimulate discussion about how all families are different, and how all families are special.

What Is a Family?

A family is a group of people who care for each other. Families can be very different.

Some families are large. They have many **family members**. Other families are very small. They have few family members.

Some people in families are **related**. This means they come from the same parent, grandparent, or great-grandparent. People can be related in many ways.

Some people in families are not related. People who are **married** are not related to each other. Children who are **adopted** are not related to their parents.

Siblings

Some families include **siblings**. Siblings are children from the same parents. Brothers are male siblings. Sisters are female siblings. Step-siblings are children from different parents.

Siblings can be older or younger than you. Siblings can look alike, or different. And siblings can even be **twins**. Twins are siblings who were born at the same time from the same parents.

Parents

Some families include parents. Parents are adults who care for children. Male parents are called fathers. Sometimes they are called dads. Female parents are called mothers. Sometimes they are called moms.

Some parents are **divorced**. Divorced parents live apart but still care for their children. Some divorced parents **remarry**. The person that a divorced parent marries becomes your **stepparent**.

Aunts and Uncles

Some families include aunts or uncles. The **siblings** of your parents are your aunts and uncles. Female siblings of a parent are called aunts. Male siblings of a parent are called uncles.

Sometimes special family friends are called aunt or uncle. They are close friends who are not **related** to the family.

Cousins

Some families include cousins. Your cousins are the children of your aunts and uncles.

Some families include many cousins. Some families include few cousins. Some families don't have any cousins at all.

Grandparents

Some families include grandparents. Grandparents are your parents' parents. Grandparents who are female are called grandmothers. Grandparents who are male are called grandfathers.

Some grandparents live with their families. Sometimes younger **family members** might help to take care of their grandparents.

Foster Parents

Foster parents are adults who care for children they are not **related** to. Foster parents help keep children safe.

Some foster parents care for the same child for a long time. Some foster parents care for a child for a short time.

Role Models

Role models are special people who help others be their best. Role models are people who set good examples for others. Role models can help you to learn things, too.

Some role models are **family members**. Other role models are special friends who are leaders. Some role models are people you've never even met!

Family Tree

Words to Know

adopted   welcomed into a new family. Many families adopt children.

divorced   no longer married

family member   person belonging to a family

married   when two people are joined by law. When two people love each other, they may decide to get married.

related   coming from the same family members. Children born from the same mother or father are related.

remarry   when adults marry again. Some parents remarry after a divorce.

sibling   brother or sister

stepparent   person a divorced parent marries

twins   two siblings born at the same time from the same mother and father

23

Index

Notes for Parents and Teachers

Before reading
Show the children the front cover of the book. Guide children in a discussion about what they know about families. Tell children that all families are different.

After reading
- Tell the children they are going to write about their families. Ask each child to describe the people in their family. Then ask them to write one thing that is special about their family. Afterwards, ask them to draw a picture of their family and label their family members.